MAD LIBS®

FIELD TRIP MAD LIBS

by Mickie Matheis

Mad Libs
An Imprint of Penguin Random House

MAD LIBS
Penguin Young Readers Group
An Imprint of Penguin Random House LLC

Mad Libs format and text copyright © 2016 by Penguin Random House LLC.
All rights reserved.

Concept created by Roger Price & Leonard Stern

Published by Mad Libs,
an imprint of Penguin Random House LLC,
345 Hudson Street, New York, New York 10014.
Printed in the USA.

ISBN 9780399539527
3 5 7 9 10 8 6 4

MAD LIBS

INSTRUCTIONS

MAD LIBS® is a game for people who don't like games! It can be played by one, two, three, four, or forty.

• RIDICULOUSLY SIMPLE DIRECTIONS

In this tablet you will find stories containing blank spaces where words are left out. One player, the READER, selects one of these stories. The READER does not tell anyone what the story is about. Instead, he/she asks the other players, the WRITERS, to give him/her words. These words are used to fill in the blank spaces in the story.

• TO PLAY

The READER asks each WRITER in turn to call out a word—an adjective or a noun or whatever the space calls for—and uses them to fill in the blank spaces in the story. The result is a MAD LIBS® game.

When the READER then reads the completed MAD LIBS® game to the other players, they will discover that they have written a story that is fantastic, screamingly funny, shocking, silly, crazy, or just plain dumb—depending upon which words each WRITER called out.

• EXAMPLE (*Before* and *After*)

" _____ !" he said _____
      EXCLAMATION   ADVERB

as he jumped into his convertible _____ and
                                                         NOUN

drove off with his _____ wife.
                          ADJECTIVE

" **OUCH** !" he said **STUPIDLY**
      EXCLAMATION   ADVERB

as he jumped into his convertible **CAT** and
                                                           NOUN

drove off with his **BRAVE** wife.
                          ADJECTIVE

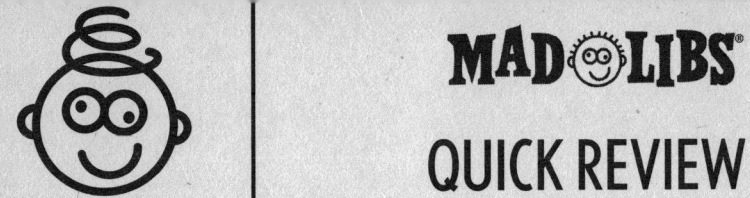

MAD LIBS®
QUICK REVIEW

In case you have forgotten what adjectives, adverbs, nouns, and verbs are, here is a quick review:

An ADJECTIVE describes something or somebody. *Lumpy*, *soft*, *ugly*, *messy*, and *short* are adjectives.

An ADVERB tells how something is done. It modifies a verb and usually ends in "ly." *Modestly*, *stupidly*, *greedily*, and *carefully* are adverbs.

A NOUN is the name of a person, place, or thing. *Sidewalk*, *umbrella*, *bridle*, *bathtub*, and *nose* are nouns.

A VERB is an action word. *Run*, *pitch*, *jump*, and *swim* are verbs. Put the verbs in past tense if the directions say PAST TENSE. *Ran*, *pitched*, *jumped*, and *swam* are verbs in the past tense.

When we ask for A PLACE, we mean any sort of place: a country or city (*Spain*, *Cleveland*) or a room (*bathroom*, *kitchen*).

An EXCLAMATION or SILLY WORD is any sort of funny sound, gasp, grunt, or outcry, like *Wow!*, *Ouch!*, *Whomp!*, *Ick!*, and *Gadzooks!*

When we ask for specific words, like a NUMBER, a COLOR, an ANIMAL, or a PART OF THE BODY, we mean a word that is one of those things, like *seven*, *blue*, *horse*, or *head*.

When we ask for a PLURAL, it means more than one. For example, *cat* pluralized is *cats*.

MAD LIBS® is fun to play with friends, but you can also play it by yourself! To begin with, DO NOT look at the story on the page below. Fill in the blanks on this page with the words called for. Then, using the words you have selected, fill in the blank spaces in the story.

Now you've created your own hilarious MAD LIBS® game!

I ♥ FIELD TRIPS

ADJECTIVE _____

A PLACE _____

VERB ENDING IN "ING" _____

NOUN _____

NOUN _____

PERSON IN ROOM _____

ADJECTIVE _____

NOUN _____

ANIMAL _____

VERB ENDING IN "ING" _____

NUMBER _____

PLURAL NOUN _____

VERB (PAST TENSE) _____

ADJECTIVE _____

PLURAL NOUN _____

ADJECTIVE _____

NOUN _____

MAD LIBS®

I ♥ FIELD TRIPS

I would rather go on a/an _____ field trip than go to school
ADJECTIVE

any day! Even just taking a trip to (the) _____ is better than
A PLACE

being stuck _____ in the classroom all day. One of my
VERB ENDING IN "ING"

favorite parts about field trips is riding in a/an _____ to our
NOUN

destination. I always choose my best _____, _____,
NOUN   _PERSON IN ROOM_

to be my seatmate. We like to pass the time playing a/an _____
ADJECTIVE

game called Road Trip Scavenger Hunt. We make a list of items to look

for during the drive, such as a/an _____ riding a motorcycle
NOUN

or a/an _____ _____ along the roadside.
ANIMAL   _VERB ENDING IN "ING"_

Field trips are fun because they teach us more about things we have

already learned in school, like how there are _____
NUMBER

_____ in our solar system or how people cooked, farmed,
PLURAL NOUN

and _____ back in the _____ days. But the
VERB (PAST TENSE)   _ADJECTIVE_

best part about taking field trips is that our _____ usually
PLURAL NOUN

don't assign any _____ homework that day—which is why if
ADJECTIVE

we could take field trips every day, I'd be the happiest _____
NOUN

in the world!

From FIELD TRIP MAD LIBS® • Copyright © 2016 by Penguin Random House LLC.

MAD LIBS® is fun to play with friends, but you can also play it by yourself! To begin with, DO NOT look at the story on the page below. Fill in the blanks on this page with the words called for. Then, using the words you have selected, fill in the blank spaces in the story.

Now you've created your own hilarious MAD LIBS® game!

RULES OF THE RIDE

CELEBRITY (MALE) _____

ADJECTIVE _____

NOUN _____

VERB ENDING IN "ING" _____

VERB _____

ADVERB _____

ADJECTIVE _____

PLURAL NOUN _____

PLURAL NOUN _____

NUMBER _____

ADJECTIVE _____

COLOR _____

PART OF THE BODY (PLURAL) _____

PLURAL NOUN _____

PART OF THE BODY _____

RULES OF THE RIDE

Whenever our bus driver for field trips is _____, our
                                              CELEBRITY (MALE)

class is in for a/an _____ time! This grumpy old _____
                        ADJECTIVE   NOUN

has strict rules to follow, such as these:

- No running or _____ up and down the aisles
                  VERB ENDING IN "ING"

  of the bus.

- Do not scream, yell, or _____ too loudly because it is
                              VERB

  _____ distracting for the driver. Use your _____
     ADVERB   ADJECTIVE

  indoor voice.

- Eating any sort of _____ is expressly prohibited!
                       PLURAL NOUN

- Do not throw anything, including paper _____.
                                            PLURAL NOUN

- Don't ask the bus driver every _____ minutes, "Are we
                                    NUMBER

  _____ yet?" This habit will make him scream and turn a
   ADJECTIVE

  bright shade of _____!
                     COLOR

- Most importantly, keep your _____ and
                                 PART OF THE BODY (PLURAL)

  _____ inside the bus at all times. Anyone caught
    PLURAL NOUN

  sticking his or her _____ out the window will be
                        PART OF THE BODY

  immediately removed from the bus.

MAD LIBS® is fun to play with friends, but you can also play it by yourself! To begin with, DO NOT look at the story on the page below. Fill in the blanks on this page with the words called for. Then, using the words you have selected, fill in the blank spaces in the story.

Now you've created your own hilarious MAD LIBS® game!

BUS BUDDY

ADJECTIVE _____

VERB ENDING IN "ING" _____

CELEBRITY _____

PART OF THE BODY _____

PLURAL NOUN _____

PLURAL NOUN _____

NOUN _____

VERB _____

ADJECTIVE _____

ANIMAL _____

ARTICLE OF CLOTHING _____

NOUN _____

A PLACE _____

VERB _____

PART OF THE BODY _____

Having a/an _____ buddy _____ next to
            ADJECTIVE   VERB ENDING IN "ING"

you on the bus is a good way to have a great field trip! First of all,

I require my bus buddy to know all the lines from every _____
                                                   CELEBRITY

movie ever made so we can recite them throughout the entire bus

ride, complete with random _____ gestures. I also appreciate
                             PART OF THE BODY

when my bus buddy packs snacks for the ride, especially things like

chocolate-covered _____ and salted _____. Of
                 PLURAL NOUN   PLURAL NOUN

course, we have to be careful that the _____ driver doesn't
                                   NOUN

see us, as we're not supposed to _____ when we're on the bus!
                                    VERB

The best bus buddies also have _____ imaginations! We'll
                              ADJECTIVE

make up stories about the flying _____ we wish we could
                               ANIMAL

have as a pet, or the sparkly _____ we'd wear as
                         ARTICLE OF CLOTHING

a superhero costume, or the giant _____ we'd live in if we
                               NOUN

owned our own private island near (the) _____. Perhaps
                                     A PLACE

the most important quality in a bus buddy is his/her size. After all,

you don't want to _____ next to someone who has such a
                     VERB

ginormous _____ that you keep falling off the seat!
         PART OF THE BODY

MAD LIBS® is fun to play with friends, but you can also play it by yourself! To begin with, DO NOT look at the story on the page below. Fill in the blanks on this page with the words called for. Then, using the words you have selected, fill in the blank spaces in the story.

Now you've created your own hilarious MAD LIBS® game!

PERMISSION SLIP

ADJECTIVE _____

VERB ENDING IN "ING" _____

NUMBER _____

NOUN _____

ADJECTIVE _____

PLURAL NOUN _____

A PLACE _____

CELEBRITY _____

PLURAL NOUN _____

PART OF THE BODY (PLURAL) _____

VERB ENDING IN "ING" _____

ADJECTIVE _____

NOUN _____

TYPE OF LIQUID _____

PLURAL NOUN _____

PLURAL NOUN _____

CELEBRITY _____

PLURAL NOUN _____

MAD LIBS®

PERMISSION SLIP

Dear Parents: Our class will be going on a/an _____ field
                                              ADJECTIVE

trip to _____ Rivers State Park next Friday. The cost
         VERB ENDING IN "ING"

of the trip is $_____, and we will be traveling to the park by
                 NUMBER

_____. The purpose of this _____ trip is to support
   NOUN   ADJECTIVE

what we've been learning in science class about the flowers, wildlife,

and _____ native to (the) _____. The trip will
     PLURAL NOUN   A PLACE

include a guided tour of the park by park ranger _____.
                                                  CELEBRITY

Be sure to remind your child to wear comfortable _____
                                                   PLURAL NOUN

on his/her _____ because he/she will be walking
            PART OF THE BODY (PLURAL)

and _____ throughout the park the entire day. Also,
     VERB ENDING IN "ING"

please be sure to pack a/an _____ lunch in a brown paper
                             ADJECTIVE

_____, including some bottled _____. We are
   NOUN   TYPE OF LIQUID

asking for several _____ to serve as chaperones on this
                    PLURAL NOUN

trip; you will oversee a group of six _____. If interested,
                                       PLURAL NOUN

please call Principal _____ at the school. Thank you in
                       CELEBRITY

advance for encouraging your children to behave like young ladies and

_____.
 PLURAL NOUN

MAD LIBS® is fun to play with friends, but you can also play it by yourself! To begin with, DO NOT look at the story on the page below. Fill in the blanks on this page with the words called for. Then, using the words you have selected, fill in the blank spaces in the story.

Now you've created your own hilarious MAD LIBS® game!

LET'S GROW TO THE FARM

NOUN _____

ANIMAL (PLURAL) _____

PERSON IN ROOM _____

EXCLAMATION _____

PART OF THE BODY _____

NOUN _____

CELEBRITY (MALE) _____

ADJECTIVE _____

NOUN _____

TYPE OF LIQUID _____

PLURAL NOUN _____

PLURAL NOUN _____

A PLACE _____

PLURAL NOUN _____

COLOR _____

PLURAL NOUN _____

NOUN _____

VERB ENDING IN "ING" _____

MAD LIBS®

LET'S GROW TO THE FARM

The moment I stepped onto the grass at Misty _____ Farm,

NOUN

I knew I was going to like it there. Just listening to the sounds of

_____ mooing, _____ oinking, and sheep

ANIMAL (PLURAL) PERSON IN ROOM

going "_____" put a smile on my _____.

EXCLAMATION PART OF THE BODY

The _____ who ran the place called himself Farmer

NOUN

_____. He showed my class how much _____

CELEBRITY (MALE) ADJECTIVE

work was required to run a farm. The first thing we learned was how

to milk a/an _____. It was amazing to see _____

NOUN TYPE OF LIQUID

come out! Afterward, we visited the chicken coop and gathered up

all the _____ that the little feathered _____

PLURAL NOUN PLURAL NOUN

had laid. Next, our class climbed into a hay wagon and was pulled all

around (the) _____ to check out the wheat, corn, and other

A PLACE

_____ growing on the farm. Lastly, the farmer took us to

PLURAL NOUN

his house where we picked juicy _____ _____

COLOR PLURAL NOUN

from a tree in his yard and had cold glasses of _____ cider.

NOUN

If I can't do _____ for a job someday, I'm going to

VERB ENDING IN "ING"

farm!

MAD LIBS® is fun to play with friends, but you can also play it by yourself! To begin with, DO NOT look at the story on the page below. Fill in the blanks on this page with the words called for. Then, using the words you have selected, fill in the blank spaces in the story.

Now you've created your own hilarious MAD LIBS® game!

OVERNIGHT FIELD TRIPS

NUMBER _____

PLURAL NOUN _____

ADJECTIVE _____

PLURAL NOUN _____

VERB ENDING IN "ING" _____

ADJECTIVE _____

ADJECTIVE _____

PART OF THE BODY _____

NOUN _____

PLURAL NOUN _____

NOUN _____

NOUN _____

MAD LIBS®

OVERNIGHT FIELD TRIPS

Taking _____ school-age _____ on the road to a
          NUMBER   PLURAL NOUN

far-off location for a class trip is no small feat! Unlike trips that are

close to school, there's a whole other set of _____ rules for
                                                 ADJECTIVE

"away" trips, including these:

- Remember to pack enough clean _____ to wear
                                        PLURAL NOUN

  each day. After all, if you're going to be _____
                                              VERB ENDING IN "ING"

  in a bus for hours, you should look and smell _____!
                                                    ADJECTIVE

- Exhibit _____ manners at meals. Be sure to neatly
            ADJECTIVE

  spread your napkin on your _____, and use your fork,
                               PART OF THE BODY

  knife, and _____ properly.
                  NOUN

- Don't ruin your hotel room by cramming furniture and

  _____ in the bathroom.
     PLURAL NOUN

- Don't try to leave your hotel room after "lights out." While

  there may not be an armed _____ stationed outside
                                  NOUN

  your door, an exhausted mom or _____ will be just as
                                      NOUN

  scary!

MAD LIBS® is fun to play with friends, but you can also play it by yourself! To begin with, DO NOT look at the story on the page below. Fill in the blanks on this page with the words called for. Then, using the words you have selected, fill in the blank spaces in the story.

Now you've created your own hilarious MAD LIBS® game!

WANTED: PARENT CHAPERONES

ADJECTIVE _____

NOUN _____

PLURAL NOUN _____

PART OF THE BODY _____

ADJECTIVE _____

ANIMAL (PLURAL) _____

PLURAL NOUN _____

VERB _____

A PLACE _____

ADJECTIVE _____

NUMBER _____

PLURAL NOUN _____

ADJECTIVE _____

PART OF THE BODY (PLURAL) _____

ADJECTIVE _____

PART OF THE BODY (PLURAL) _____

ADJECTIVE _____

VERB _____

MAD LIBS®
WANTED:
PARENT CHAPERONES

Are you daring, adventurous, and _____? Does the thought
_____ADJECTIVE_____

of driving in a stuffy, cramped _____ with a bunch of loud,
_____NOUN

boisterous _____ make your _____ beat with
____PLURAL NOUN____ ____PART OF THE BODY____

excitement? Can you picture yourself herding rowdy, _____
____ADJECTIVE____

children like a pack of pygmy _____? If so, then *you* could
____ANIMAL (PLURAL)____

be a field trip chaperone! Join our team of ultra-responsible adult

_____ charged with making sure that students *walk*, not
___PLURAL NOUN___

_____, around a zoo, a museum, (the) _____, or
___VERB___ ____A PLACE____

whatever location their _____ teacher has selected for the
____ADJECTIVE____

field trip. While previous experience is not required, candidates who

can manage up to _____ _____ at any given time
____NUMBER____ ____PLURAL NOUN____

while maintaining a/an _____ sense of humor are preferred.
____ADJECTIVE____

Those with eyes in the back of their _____ will be
____PART OF THE BODY (PLURAL)____

given top consideration. And while there's no salary, the joy of seeing

_____ expressions on the kids' _____ as
____ADJECTIVE____ ____PART OF THE BODY (PLURAL)____

they learn something new will be reward enough! If this sounds like

a/an _____ job for you, _____ today for an application!
____ADJECTIVE____ ____VERB____

MAD LIBS® is fun to play with friends, but you can also play it by yourself! To begin with, DO NOT look at the story on the page below. Fill in the blanks on this page with the words called for. Then, using the words you have selected, fill in the blank spaces in the story.

Now you've created your own hilarious MAD LIBS® game!

FORGETTABLE FIELD TRIPS

ADJECTIVE _____

PART OF THE BODY _____

ADJECTIVE _____

VERB _____

PLURAL NOUN _____

PLURAL NOUN _____

ADJECTIVE _____

PART OF THE BODY (PLURAL) _____

ADVERB _____

NOUN _____

CELEBRITY _____

VERB ENDING IN "ING" _____

ADVERB _____

VERB (PAST TENSE) _____

PLURAL NOUN _____

VERB ENDING IN "ING" _____

ADJECTIVE _____

ADJECTIVE _____

MAD LIBS®

FORGETTABLE FIELD TRIPS

Not all field trips are fun, _____ adventures. Some have left
ADJECTIVE

me shaking my _____ and wondering what in the world
PART OF THE BODY

my _____ teacher was thinking. For example, one time my
ADJECTIVE

class had to _____ along the highway, picking up crumpled
VERB

_____, moldy _____, and other _____
PLURAL NOUN   PLURAL NOUN   ADJECTIVE

garbage that made us turn up our _____ in
PART OF THE BODY (PLURAL)

disgust. It was _____ gross! Another time, we went to
ADVERB

a/an _____ hardware store where an employee wearing
NOUN

a name tag that said "Hi! My name is _____" showed us
CELEBRITY

pieces of wood, paint samples, and tools for building, gardening, and

_____. It was _____ boring! And another
VERB ENDING IN "ING"   ADVERB

time, we _____ for hours at a local funeral home and
VERB (PAST TENSE)

learned how dead _____ were prepared for burial. I still have
PLURAL NOUN

nightmares where I wake up trembling and _____!
VERB ENDING IN "ING"

The next time one of these _____ field trips is planned, I'll be
ADJECTIVE

calling in _____!
ADJECTIVE

MAD LIBS® is fun to play with friends, but you can also play it by yourself! To begin with, DO NOT look at the story on the page below. Fill in the blanks on this page with the words called for. Then, using the words you have selected, fill in the blank spaces in the story.

Now you've created your own hilarious MAD LIBS® game!

BEST. FIELD TRIP. EVER.

A PLACE _____

CELEBRITY (MALE) _____

VERB _____

PLURAL NOUN _____

PART OF THE BODY _____

TYPE OF LIQUID _____

NUMBER _____

SILLY WORD _____

PART OF THE BODY (PLURAL) _____

ADJECTIVE _____

NOUN _____

NOUN _____

PLURAL NOUN _____

ADJECTIVE _____

PERSON IN ROOM _____

SAME PERSON IN ROOM _____

PART OF THE BODY _____

SILLY WORD _____

ADJECTIVE _____

MAD LIBS

BEST. FIELD TRIP. EVER.

Our class was visiting the Bank of (the) _____ to
A PLACE

learn about money. As we stood there, waiting for security guard

_____ to unlock the door to the vault so we could
CELEBRITY (MALE)

_____ inside, three masked _____ ran into the
VERB   PLURAL NOUN

bank. They blasted the guard squarely in the _____ with
PART OF THE BODY

_____ from a water gun and knocked him to the ground.
TYPE OF LIQUID

Then they ran into the vault and stuffed bags full of $_____
NUMBER

bills. "_____! Get down on your _____!"
SILLY WORD   PART OF THE BODY (PLURAL)

one of the _____ robbers yelled at us. Then they ran out
ADJECTIVE

the front door, jumped into a getaway _____, and sped off.
NOUN

Back inside the bank, the security _____ called the police to
NOUN

report the theft of thousands of _____. I could hear the
PLURAL NOUN

_____ sound of a police siren getting closer. "_____!
ADJECTIVE   PERSON IN ROOM

_____!" a voice said into my _____. "We're
SAME PERSON IN ROOM   PART OF THE BODY

here." _____, I had fallen asleep on the bus! The most exciting
SILLY WORD

field trip of my life had only been a/an _____ dream!
ADJECTIVE

MAD LIBS® is fun to play with friends, but you can also play it by yourself! To begin with, DO NOT look at the story on the page below. Fill in the blanks on this page with the words called for. Then, using the words you have selected, fill in the blank spaces in the story.

Now you've created your own hilarious MAD LIBS® game!

DREAM TRIPS

PERSON IN ROOM _____

PART OF THE BODY _____

ADJECTIVE _____

NOUN _____

A PLACE _____

NUMBER _____

CELEBRITY _____

VERB ENDING IN "ING" _____

PLURAL NOUN _____

TYPE OF LIQUID _____

NOUN _____

NOUN _____

A PLACE _____

TYPE OF FOOD _____

ANIMAL _____

A PLACE _____

TYPE OF FOOD _____

PLURAL NOUN _____

MAD LIBS

DREAM TRIPS

When the teacher asked for suggestions for class field trips,

_____ raised a/an _____ and proposed these
PERSON IN ROOM   PART OF THE BODY

far-fetched but super-_____ ideas:
                          ADJECTIVE

- Charter a/an _____ to fly the class to (the)
                      NOUN

  _____ for a/an _____-course meal prepared by
    A PLACE   NUMBER

  _____.
    CELEBRITY

- Go scuba-_____ with dolphins, stingrays,
              VERB ENDING IN "ING"

  and other undersea _____ in the crystal-clear
                          PLURAL NOUN

  _____ of the _____ Ocean.
    TYPE OF LIQUID   NOUN

- Travel to a private _____ off the coast of (the)
                            NOUN

  _____ where students could Jet Ski, yacht, and sip
    A PLACE

  _____-flavored lemonade all day.
    TYPE OF FOOD

- Go _____-back riding around the remote jungles of
        ANIMAL

  (the) _____.
          A PLACE

- Rent out the local ice-cream parlor and spend the afternoon

  eating _____-flavored ice cream with whipped
            TYPE OF FOOD

  _____ and sprinkles on top.
    PLURAL NOUN

MAD LIBS® is fun to play with friends, but you can also play it by yourself! To begin with, DO NOT look at the story on the page below. Fill in the blanks on this page with the words called for. Then, using the words you have selected, fill in the blank spaces in the story.

Now you've created your own hilarious MAD LIBS® game!

BROWN BAG LUNCH SPECIAL

NOUN _____

NOUN _____

PLURAL NOUN _____

TYPE OF FOOD _____

TYPE OF LIQUID _____

VERB _____

PART OF THE BODY _____

PLURAL NOUN _____

NOUN _____

ADJECTIVE _____

PERSON IN ROOM _____

NOUN _____

NOUN _____

NOUN _____

CELEBRITY _____

TYPE OF FOOD _____

ADJECTIVE _____

PART OF THE BODY _____

MAD LIBS®
BROWN BAG
LUNCH SPECIAL

Remember to pack lunches in a brown paper _____ when
NOUN

your child is going on a field trip. One of the most popular bagged

lunches is a peanut butter and _____ sandwich, sliced
NOUN

_____, and _____-chip cookies. A smart way to
PLURAL NOUN   TYPE OF FOOD

keep the lunch cold is to freeze a bottle of _____ the night
TYPE OF LIQUID

before the trip. It serves as an ice pack until it's time to _____.
VERB

Don't forget to include a napkin so that your child can wipe his or her

_____. Some moms and _____ like to make a packed
PART OF THE BODY   PLURAL NOUN

lunch special for their little _____. You could tuck a small note
NOUN

in the bag that says "Have a/an _____ day, _____—I
ADJECTIVE   PERSON IN ROOM

love you with all my _____!" Or you could liven up the lunch
NOUN

by drawing games of tic-tac-_____ on the bag or creating
NOUN

a lunch-themed word search with words like "sandwich," "drink,"

"_____," and more! Or you could decorate the bag with
NOUN

pictures of _____ or stuff _____-scented stickers
CELEBRITY   TYPE OF FOOD

inside. Any of these _____ ideas will bring a smile to your
ADJECTIVE

child's _____!
PART OF THE BODY

From FIELD TRIP MAD LIBS® • Copyright © 2016 by Penguin Random House LLC.

MAD LIBS® is fun to play with friends, but you can also play it by yourself! To begin with, DO NOT look at the story on the page below. Fill in the blanks on this page with the words called for. Then, using the words you have selected, fill in the blank spaces in the story.

Now you've created your own hilarious MAD LIBS® game!

FIELD TRIP ETIQUETTE

ADJECTIVE _____

ADJECTIVE _____

PLURAL NOUN _____

VERB _____

NOUN _____

VERB ENDING IN "ING" _____

VERB _____

PART OF THE BODY _____

PLURAL NOUN _____

PART OF THE BODY (PLURAL) _____

NOUN _____

VERB _____

NOUN _____

NOUN _____

SILLY WORD _____

MAD LIBS®

FIELD TRIP ETIQUETTE

Students are expected to be on their most _____ behavior
ADJECTIVE

during a field trip so a/an _____ time can be had by all. Our
ADJECTIVE

class rules are as follows:

- Stay with the other _____ in your group as well as
PLURAL NOUN

  your chaperone. When using the "buddy system," make sure

  you always _____ with your _____.
VERB   NOUN

- No talking or _____ when the tour guide is
VERB ENDING IN "ING"

  trying to _____.
VERB

- If you have a question, raise your _____.
PART OF THE BODY

- Don't touch any _____ on display unless you are
PLURAL NOUN

  given permission.

- Keep your hands and _____ to yourself.
PART OF THE BODY (PLURAL)

- If you get separated from your _____, don't
NOUN

  panic. Calmly _____ where you are until an adult
VERB

  _____ comes to find you.
NOUN

- Be courteous to the tour _____ and say things like
NOUN

  "please," "thank you," and "_____."
SILLY WORD

MAD LIBS® is fun to play with friends, but you can also play it by yourself! To begin with, DO NOT look at the story on the page below. Fill in the blanks on this page with the words called for. Then, using the words you have selected, fill in the blank spaces in the story.

Now you've created your own hilarious MAD LIBS® game!

THE NATURAL HISTORY MUSEUM

A PLACE _____

PLURAL NOUN _____

PLURAL NOUN _____

VERB ENDING IN "ING" _____

ANIMAL (PLURAL) _____

ADJECTIVE _____

PLURAL NOUN _____

ADJECTIVE _____

TYPE OF LIQUID _____

PART OF THE BODY _____

ANIMAL (PLURAL) _____

NUMBER _____

NOUN _____

A PLACE _____

PERSON IN ROOM _____

VERB _____

ADJECTIVE _____

VERB _____

MAD LIBS
THE NATURAL HISTORY MUSEUM

Teachers, one of the best places in all of (the) _____ to
A PLACE

take your class on a field trip is the Natural History Museum. The

museum offers unique experiences for _____ of all ages.
PLURAL NOUN

Whether your students are learning about the Earth, the solar system,

dinosaurs, mammals, _____, or _____
PLURAL NOUN   VERB ENDING IN "ING"

_____, the Natural History Museum has _____
ANIMAL (PLURAL)   ADJECTIVE

displays and interactive _____ to support your classroom
PLURAL NOUN

teachings. It's a one-of-a-kind environment to explore and learn about

the _____ natural world and our place in it. New exhibits
ADJECTIVE

include an actual working volcano from which _____ erupts,
TYPE OF LIQUID

a hands-on enclosure where you can come face-to-_____
PART OF THE BODY

with live _____, a/an _____-year-old fossilized
ANIMAL (PLURAL)   NUMBER

_____ found on an archaeological dig in (the) _____,
NOUN   A PLACE

and _____, a skeleton of a three-million-year-old human
PERSON IN ROOM

ancestor. Come to explore, stay to _____! You'll have such
VERB

a/an _____ time visiting the Natural History Museum, you
ADJECTIVE

won't ever want to _____!
VERB

MAD LIBS® is fun to play with friends, but you can also play it by yourself! To begin with, DO NOT look at the story on the page below. Fill in the blanks on this page with the words called for. Then, using the words you have selected, fill in the blank spaces in the story.

Now you've created your own hilarious MAD LIBS® game!

THEATER ADVENTURES

ADJECTIVE _____

VERB ENDING IN "ING" _____

NOUN _____

NOUN _____

CELEBRITY (MALE) _____

NOUN _____

VERB _____

NUMBER _____

ADJECTIVE _____

ADJECTIVE _____

PART OF THE BODY (PLURAL) _____

VERB _____

NOUN _____

VERB (PAST TENSE) _____

PLURAL NOUN _____

VERB _____

PART OF THE BODY _____

ADJECTIVE _____

MAD LIBS

THEATER ADVENTURES

On the way to see the _____ stage musical _____
                        ADJECTIVE   VERB ENDING IN "ING"

in the Rain at the Little _____ Playhouse, our _____
                            NOUN   NOUN

teacher, Mr. _____, quizzed the class on theater terms:
              CELEBRITY (MALE)

- To **audition** means to show the casting _____
                                             NOUN

  how well you can _____. You'll recite up to
                    VERB

  _____ lines from a/an _____ play while making
   NUMBER   ADJECTIVE

  _____ facial expressions and gesturing wildly with
   ADJECTIVE

  your _____.
        PART OF THE BODY (PLURAL)

- A **callback** is the opportunity to _____ for the casting
                                        VERB

  _____ a second time because you _____
   NOUN   VERB (PAST TENSE)

  so well the first time.

- A **curtain call** is when the _____ who acted in the
                                  PLURAL NOUN

  play come back out onto the stage and take bows while audience

  members clap and _____ with appreciation.
                    VERB

- "Break a/an _____" is an odd but _____ way
               PART OF THE BODY   ADJECTIVE

  of saying "good luck" to an actor.

MAD LIBS® is fun to play with friends, but you can also play it by yourself! To begin with, DO NOT look at the story on the page below. Fill in the blanks on this page with the words called for. Then, using the words you have selected, fill in the blank spaces in the story.

Now you've created your own hilarious MAD LIBS® game!

WELCOME TO WASHINGTON, DC

A PLACE _____

PLURAL NOUN _____

NOUN _____

ANIMAL (PLURAL) _____

NOUN _____

PLURAL NOUN _____

ADJECTIVE _____

CELEBRITY _____

VERB ENDING IN "ING" _____

PERSON IN ROOM _____

ADJECTIVE _____

NOUN _____

COLOR _____

PERSON IN ROOM _____

ADJECTIVE _____

VERB _____

PLURAL NOUN _____

MAD LIBS®
WELCOME TO
WASHINGTON, DC

Visiting (the) _____, the capital of the United States, is an
<u>A PLACE</u>

amazing way to teach students about our country! This bustling city

is home to many national monuments, memorials, museums, and

other _____ of historical significance. Get ready to explore
<u>PLURAL NOUN</u>

the National Air and _____ Museum, which highlights
<u>NOUN</u>

America's journey of sending _____ into space. Pay your
<u>ANIMAL (PLURAL)</u>

respects at the _____ War Memorial, which remembers the
<u>NOUN</u>

_____ that served in that _____ conflict. Grab
<u>PLURAL NOUN</u> <u>ADJECTIVE</u>

photos at the _____ Memorial, which honors the leader
<u>CELEBRITY</u>

of the _____ movement, and the _____
<u>VERB ENDING IN "ING"</u> <u>PERSON IN ROOM</u>

Monument, which commemorates the pioneering works of this

_____ _____. The grand finale is a private tour
<u>ADJECTIVE</u> <u>NOUN</u>

of the _____ House, led by the head of the Secret Service,
<u>COLOR</u>

Agent _____. Previous students have called this part of
<u>PERSON IN ROOM</u>

the trip "unforgettable," "once in a lifetime," and "_____."
<u>ADJECTIVE</u>

Who knows? Maybe someday you'll return to Washington, DC, to

_____ there—as president of the United _____!
<u>VERB</u> <u>PLURAL NOUN</u>

MAD LIBS® is fun to play with friends, but you can also play it by yourself! To begin with, DO NOT look at the story on the page below. Fill in the blanks on this page with the words called for. Then, using the words you have selected, fill in the blank spaces in the story.

Now you've created your own hilarious MAD LIBS® game!

INTERVIEW WITH A ZOOKEEPER

PERSON IN ROOM (MALE) _____

PLURAL NOUN _____

PLURAL NOUN _____

NOUN _____

NOUN _____

COLOR _____

NOUN _____

CELEBRITY _____

NOUN _____

PLURAL NOUN _____

A PLACE _____

ADJECTIVE _____

NUMBER _____

PART OF THE BODY (PLURAL) _____

VERB _____

TYPE OF LIQUID _____

VERB _____

ADJECTIVE _____

MAD LIBS
INTERVIEW WITH
A ZOOKEEPER

This is Suzy Woods of ZOO-TV with _____, aka
<u>PERSON IN ROOM (MALE)</u>

"Jungle Genius," here at the _____ of the Wild Animal
<u>PLURAL NOUN</u>

Park. He teaches facts to kids about the different mammals, reptiles,

and _____ from around the world. I asked him to tell me
<u>PLURAL NOUN</u>

which _____ at the park he liked best.
<u>NOUN</u>

Suzy: What's your favorite _____ here at the zoo?
<u>NOUN</u>

Genius: It's a two-ton _____ _____ named
<u>COLOR</u>   <u>NOUN</u>

_____. It's a rare species of _____ found only in the
<u>CELEBRITY</u>   <u>NOUN</u>

deepest, darkest _____ of (the) _____.
<u>PLURAL NOUN</u>   <u>A PLACE</u>

Suzy: What should we know about this _____ creature?
<u>ADJECTIVE</u>

Genius: It has gills, _____ legs, and wings resembling
<u>NUMBER</u>

_____, meaning it can _____ in
<u>PART OF THE BODY (PLURAL)</u>   <u>VERB</u>

_____, walk on the ground, and _____ through
<u>TYPE OF LIQUID</u>   <u>VERB</u>

the air! Who needs a/an _____ dog or a cat for a pet when you
<u>ADJECTIVE</u>

can have one of these?

MAD LIBS® is fun to play with friends, but you can also play it by yourself! To begin with, DO NOT look at the story on the page below. Fill in the blanks on this page with the words called for. Then, using the words you have selected, fill in the blank spaces in the story.

Now you've created your own hilarious MAD LIBS® game!

FIRE STATION FUN

NOUN _____

PERSON IN ROOM (MALE) _____

VEHICLE _____

PLURAL NOUN _____

ADVERB _____

PART OF THE BODY (PLURAL) _____

NOUN _____

PLURAL NOUN _____

ARTICLE OF CLOTHING _____

CELEBRITY (MALE) _____

VERB (PAST TENSE) _____

ADJECTIVE _____

PLURAL NOUN _____

TYPE OF LIQUID _____

NOUN _____

NOUN _____

VERB _____

ADJECTIVE _____

MAD LIBS®

FIRE STATION FUN

When I was a little _____, my favorite field trip was visiting

NOUN

the fire station!

Firefighter _____ showed my class the big _____

PERSON IN ROOM (MALE) VEHICLE

that the firefighters drove. He turned on the flashing red

_____ and even sounded the alarm. It was so _____

PLURAL NOUN ADVERB

loud that I had to cover my _____! Another

PART OF THE BODY (PLURAL)

firefighter came out dressed in her _____-fighting gear, which

NOUN

included boots, a smoke mask, rubber _____, and a

PLURAL NOUN

protective _____. Afterward, Chief _____ took

ARTICLE OF CLOTHING CELEBRITY (MALE)

us on a tour of the fire station. We saw where the firefighters ate,

slept, and _____. There was an exercise room for the

VERB (PAST TENSE)

firefighters to use to stay strong and _____ in order to climb

ADJECTIVE

up _____ and haul the heavy hoses that spray

PLURAL NOUN

_____. The chief taught us to always make sure the

TYPE OF LIQUID

_____ detectors in our houses worked and never play with a

NOUN

lighted _____. He also showed us how to stop, drop, and

NOUN

_____, because it's always better to be safe than _____!

VERB ADJECTIVE

MAD LIBS® is fun to play with friends, but you can also play it by yourself! To begin with, DO NOT look at the story on the page below. Fill in the blanks on this page with the words called for. Then, using the words you have selected, fill in the blank spaces in the story.

Now you've created your own hilarious MAD LIBS® game!

AFTER THE AQUARIUM: A FIELD TRIP ESSAY

PERSON IN ROOM _____

A PLACE _____

TYPE OF LIQUID _____

VERB _____

ADJECTIVE _____

ADVERB _____

NOUN _____

PLURAL NOUN _____

PLURAL NOUN _____

COLOR _____

TYPE OF LIQUID _____

NOUN _____

TYPE OF LIQUID _____

PLURAL NOUN _____

PLURAL NOUN _____

NOUN _____

ADJECTIVE _____

VERB _____

MAD LIBS®
AFTER THE AQUARIUM:
A FIELD TRIP ESSAY

Ocean Life, by _____
                    PERSON IN ROOM

Oceans cover more than 70 percent of (the) _____'s surface
                                              A PLACE

and contain about 97 percent of the Earth's supply of _____.
                                                        TYPE OF LIQUID

There are many fascinating creatures that _____ in the oceans,
                                              VERB

with _____ features and _____ amazing abilities. For
       ADJECTIVE   ADVERB

example, the blue whale is the largest _____ ever to have lived
                                          NOUN

and weighs close to two hundred tons, which is roughly the equivalent

of fifty full-grown African _____. The octopus has eight
                             PLURAL NOUN

long _____, called tentacles, and can shoot out _____
      PLURAL NOUN   COLOR

_____ when a predator threatens it. A puffer-_____
TYPE OF LIQUID   NOUN

is a fish that can quickly swallow enough _____ to inflate
                                            TYPE OF LIQUID

its own body so large, no other _____ can eat it. Crabs are
                                  PLURAL NOUN

very lucky sea-_____ because whenever they lose a claw,
               PLURAL NOUN

another _____ grows in its place. These are just some of the
          NOUN

_____ facts I learned about ocean life during my trip to the
ADJECTIVE

aquarium. I can't wait to _____ there again!
                            VERB

MAD LIBS® is fun to play with friends, but you can also play it by yourself! To begin with, DO NOT look at the story on the page below. Fill in the blanks on this page with the words called for. Then, using the words you have selected, fill in the blank spaces in the story.

Now you've created your own hilarious MAD LIBS® game!

CHAPERONE SURVIVAL TIPS

NOUN _____

ADJECTIVE _____

PART OF THE BODY _____

VERB _____

PLURAL NOUN _____

PART OF THE BODY (PLURAL) _____

TYPE OF LIQUID _____

NOUN _____

PART OF THE BODY _____

NOUN _____

PART OF THE BODY _____

NUMBER _____

PART OF THE BODY _____

PERSON IN ROOM _____

NOUN _____

MAD LIBS®

CHAPERONE SURVIVAL TIPS

Any adult _____ who volunteers to chaperone a field trip is

NOUN

to be congratulated for their _____ bravery. It's *not* a job

ADJECTIVE

for the faint of _____! Here are some tips from the pros to

PART OF THE BODY

ensure you not only survive, but _____!

VERB

- Wear comfortable walking _____ on your

PLURAL NOUN

  _____.

PART OF THE BODY (PLURAL)

- Stay hydrated with _____, and snack often.

TYPE OF LIQUID

- The bus ride will have the deafening noise level of a/an

  _____ concert, and the seats will (literally) be a pain

NOUN

  in your _____. Take a headache pill in advance—

PART OF THE BODY

  or just plan to drive your own _____.

NOUN

- Do frequent _____-counts to ensure you start and

PART OF THE BODY

  finish with _____ kids.

NUMBER

- Last but not least, keep a/an _____ on any student

PART OF THE BODY

  named _____. A/An _____ with that name

PERSON IN ROOM   NOUN

  always seems to be trouble!

MAD LIBS® is fun to play with friends, but you can also play it by yourself! To begin with, DO NOT look at the story on the page below. Fill in the blanks on this page with the words called for. Then, using the words you have selected, fill in the blank spaces in the story.

Now you've created your own hilarious MAD LIBS® game!

CLASSIC FIELD TRIP MOVIES

PLURAL NOUN _____

NOUN _____

ADJECTIVE _____

NOUN _____

PLURAL NOUN _____

ADJECTIVE _____

PERSON IN ROOM _____

ADJECTIVE _____

NOUN _____

CELEBRITY _____

VERB ENDING IN "ING" _____

PERSON IN ROOM (MALE) _____

TYPE OF FOOD _____

NOUN _____

NOUN _____

ADJECTIVE _____

NOUN _____

CELEBRITY (MALE) _____

MAD LIBS®

CLASSIC FIELD TRIP MOVIES

Let's grab a bucket of buttered _____ and curl up on the
$\qquad$ PLURAL NOUN

_____ to watch these _____ field trip movies that
NOUN ADJECTIVE

every school-age _____ should see:
NOUN

Prehistoric Park: A class of science-minded junior _____
PLURAL NOUN

visit an ancient forest where _____ dinosaurs such as the
ADJECTIVE

_____-asaurus roam free.
PERSON IN ROOM

Overnight at the _____ *Museum*: Students camp out at the
ADJECTIVE

Historical _____ Museum and discover that wax figures of
NOUN

famous historical people, such as Pocahontas, Christopher Columbus,

Teddy Roosevelt, and _____, come back to life at night and
CELEBRITY

spend hours singing, dancing, and _____ throughout the
VERB ENDING IN "ING"

museum.

_____ *and the* _____ *Factory*: A young
PERSON IN ROOM (MALE)   TYPE OF FOOD

_____ finds a winning golden _____ that allows him
NOUN   NOUN

and his class to tour the elusive, _____ factory owned by an
ADJECTIVE

eccentric _____ named Mr. _____.
NOUN   CELEBRITY (MALE)

MAD LIBS® is fun to play with friends, but you can also play it by yourself! To begin with, DO NOT look at the story on the page below. Fill in the blanks on this page with the words called for. Then, using the words you have selected, fill in the blank spaces in the story.

Now you've created your own hilarious MAD LIBS® game!

FIELD TRIPPIN':
TEACHER FEEDBACK

PLURAL NOUN _____

VERB ENDING IN "ING" _____

PLURAL NOUN _____

PLURAL NOUN _____

NUMBER _____

ANIMAL (PLURAL) _____

TYPE OF FOOD (PLURAL) _____

NOUN _____

ADJECTIVE _____

VERB _____

NUMBER _____

TYPE OF LIQUID _____

PERSON IN ROOM (MALE) _____

TYPE OF LIQUID _____

PART OF THE BODY _____

PLURAL NOUN _____

VERB ENDING IN "ING" _____

ADJECTIVE _____

Dear Parents:

I am sending home this note to tell you how proud I was of your

_____ today on our field trip to the Science Museum! I was
PLURAL NOUN

particularly impressed with them during the Imagine an Invention

exhibit. They put on their _____ caps and came up
VERB ENDING IN "ING"

with some genius _____! One student used a spool of
PLURAL NOUN

_____, _____ miniature _____,
PLURAL NOUN   NUMBER   ANIMAL (PLURAL)

paper clips, and some day-old _____ to fashion a
TYPE OF FOOD (PLURAL)

jet-propelled _____. And the students had a ton of
NOUN

_____ fun at the Ocean Exhibit, a giant tank where they
ADJECTIVE

could splash, play, and _____ in over _____ gallons of
VERB   NUMBER

_____. There was one minor mishap where
TYPE OF LIQUID

_____ drenched the poor tour guide with
PERSON IN ROOM (MALE)

a/an _____ cannon and soaked her from head to
TYPE OF LIQUID

_____! Be sure to ask your _____ about the trip
PART OF THE BODY   PLURAL NOUN

tonight when you're _____ around the dinner table.
VERB ENDING IN "ING"

They had a/an _____ time!
ADJECTIVE

Join the millions of Mad Libs fans creating wacky and wonderful stories on our apps!

Download Mad Libs today!